THE YIELD

THE YIELD

SUE WOOTTON

OTAGO

To Doug

Published by Otago University Press
Level 1, 398 Cumberland Street
Dunedin, New Zealand
university.press@otago.ac.nz
www.otago.ac.nz/press

First published 2017
Copyright © Sue Wootton

Editor: Emma Neale
Design/layout: Fiona Moffat

Front cover: *Apples on Box* (detail) by Neil Driver. Acrylic on board.

Printed in New Zealand by Printing.com, Wellington

Amazed, morning after morning
by the yielding.

– Jack Gilbert, 'Singing in my difficult mountains',
Collected Poems, New York: Knopf, 2014.

CONTENTS

Wild

Measure my wild. Down to my last leaf,
my furled, my desiccated. This deciduousness,
this bloom. Calculate my xylem levels,
my spore count, fungal, scarlet
in a bluebell glade. Whoosh,
where the foliage closes on a great cat.
Test me: how many tigers in my jungle,
how many lions at roam? Map my rivers,
deltas, estuaries. Mollusc, whelk, worm.
Monitor my silt. Do I have spoonbills,
high-stepping and watchful over the darting fish?
Rainfall on pines. Dappled sunlight
in my dells. Under moss, the fallen log, under
the log the hibernating hedgehog. Late my dates,
or soon? Return of the albatross, godwits
gathering. What clouds me, shifts,
but: indigo thunder-stack, pink wisp. Count the mice.
What will survive me, O my cockroaches, O my lice?
Scaffold me with metal, cage me in glass, tube me,
needle me, fill me, flush me. Saline solution:
the ocean. Oxygen therapy: the sky.
Mineral deficiency: socks off. Soil. Dark
rot, eye-less wriggle, while the roots seek, seek.
Undiagnosable, that ticklish insect.
Mountain peak speak only snow, and thus
I am diminished; thus I rest in my pulse. Sweet
heart. Examine my yearn, and treat it with trees.
Un-pane me. Wilden my outlook.
Membrane animal, skin mammal under the osmosis moon.
Allow my tides. All this to say, in love we nest, and on Earth.

A behoovement

'Icebergs behoove the soul' – Elizabeth Bishop, 'The imaginary iceberg'

Seeks ceaselessly a spectrum space, one third afloat
and flashing in the squawking skyworld,
sculptured spectacle, sailing bright white

spectre-ship, two thirds submerged beneath
what splashes on the skin, in stately counterweight
to being awake: blue realm articulate in creaks and cracks
and booms. Prussian, midnight, cuttlefish, forget-
me-not. Behoven to its own and constant re-assemblage.
What is the soul to do, if the icebergs melt?

Palaces

The gondolier had fallen silent. He leaned
more weight on the pole with each pass,
scanning the darkening water beyond the prow

for his next mark, hitching himself to the slight lift
as the hull flowed forward of the oar.
In room after room lamps were being lit.

A dining table, silver-set with cutlery
and candelabra; a bowl of roses
on a mantelpiece above a marble hearth.

Sky-blue ceilings with powder-puff clouds.
A frieze of cherubs; a frieze of grapes. Cello
and a high-backed wooden chair. Chaise,

a tented paperback upon it. Whole walls
of tapestries; whole walls of books. Glimpse
of an elaborate gilded frame, a youthful face

within it, centuries old. Glimpse of a girl in jeans
gazing at herself in a mirror. The tableau floated past.
Why does it come back now? It's dusk

and all along this street, behind the fences, rooms
are being lit by people propelling themselves
through their lives.   *Slow, slow*, I want to call,

and I wanted – but brocades were being drawn across
the palace windows, and the gondolier's eye was on
the dock, and our day gliding in a myth was almost done.

The needlework, the polishing

I like an empty church, forgive me. I like
a heavy door you have to push until it gives.
I like the onrush of the smell of must,
the sound of my sole self stepping up the aisle.
I'll always like the way the door behind me
closing echoes. Goes. I like the way
the after-echo opens still. The needlework,
the polishing. A rose window, sure, and if
stained motes could circulate shaft-lit
high up at Sunday pace, O please. Ever
dust-dance lift mine eyes above the pulpit
while I perch at pew. Flat cushions laid out
dead on cold, hard seats with cold, hard backs.
The kneeling rail. I kneel. I quietly rail.

Mammatus

They bulged, knife-pasted to the morning sky,
ink-veined, creamy, oil-swirl thick. When
did they form? The air was tense and warm.
Beneath, we drove, or took the bus, or walked
to work, or carried baskets out to peg the socks.
We looked up often. They pushed their dugs on us.
They didn't budge. Not vaporous puffs,
but solid, set, and sculpted, marble-streaked
and marvellous. Or mad. This canopy
might burn and wheel, might split,
might vomit flapping cawing smuts, might spew
its pent and rotted milk to pit our pretty town.
What pressed? What pressed? We carried on, routine.
We continued, eyes averted now. Obscene.

Mammatus: a rare formation of downward-bulging clouds

Picnic

The wicker hamper, in which was wedged the tea thermos, the Mountain Man Escape espresso kit, a smoked chicken salad with a pomegranate salsa, individual retro prawn cocktails with Highlander mayonnaise and a sprig of parsley, pumpkin wild rice and glass noodle risotto, home-fizzed cork-bottled lemonade, a tan-brown bubble-topped gooseberry pie, baked fresh (still warm) from last year's gooseberries retrieved from the back of the freezer. A tartan rug. The kids, the sporks, the spoodle. Fishing rods, dinghy, double kayak, tennis racquets, whitebait net, the bicycles, and off we went. *Poop poop!*

A sour breeze blew from the curdled sea. No one would budge. Lucy whined. Hugh snatched her My Little Glitter Pony, threw it out. It landed in a puddle on its side, mud-splattered belly-bloat and rigid legs. Ruined, she screamed. Through teeth calmly I suggested a spot of fishing, cockles for bait, *tra-la*, but rapidly the tide was gobbling the mudflats. We let the spoodle off its leash and had the kids walk into the wind. Lucy sobbed for the pony. Hugh wished aloud for technology. The spoodle lolloped away and rolled in something smelly.

You have to apologise, she said.   I'm sorry.

Oh, it was quite a picnic. Home we drove, and stopped at Hell's Pizza for a bite. Sand on the skin. Reptilian. Sliding the fingernails under the grains, peeling off quartz for days.

Autumn voltage

The kids come back from the documentary
about religion laughing

uproariously at the fundamentalists
we're all laughing   it's side-splitting   it's

absurd
then suddenly

appalling   we've gone
righteous   where are our

words for mystery if not
in religion I ask

but the kids are dismissive
and convulsed and very

scientific even if one has the Coloseum
confused with the Cathedral   then

the sun in autumn voltage
pops a pod   and

ping!   another
yellow pellet fires   and

O my god! they cry in unison
look at all these seeds!

Jar

With

holding comes trust, for

it must not be dropped, nor fear

to be dropped. Small, blue, crazed. Pretty

cheap. But possibly antique. Possibly valuable. Yes,

pretty common hope. Chosen for someone the giver loved,

no, for someone the giver wanted to love, dearly, for someone

who would dearly love the right jar, the right dear antique

jar, yes, for someone about whom the giver harboured ginger

thoughts, and *that's* what lingers in the belly of this

jar, and *that's* the scent that rises when

the lid is lifted: withholding.

How to paint a weeping woman

Not by painting tears, exactly.
Nor cheeks, nor face, nor even woman
(leaning on the table, making a hide of her fingers).

The café is a charcoal blur, a vortex of clatter,
the barista's wrist a falling swirl of steam.
Paint that.

And her? Estuaries creep across her bony shorelines.
She rows a red boat through the black river.
Butterfish swim under the hull. Oak oars dip, creak, drip.

She is visited by migratory birds.
Her clavicles taste of salt.
Sough, pines. Thud, cones.

       If you can haul on your brush.
       If it pulls you through.

!
FORD

At last we come to it, the ford
we were warned of, a dip in the gravel road

they said might be impassable
in mid-July. A warning that seems laughable –

the riverbed is dry and hard
as made for speed. Above, the peaks

soar summer-brown and snowless.
The guy back there where we filled up

did say there'd been no night frosts yet,
no pre-dawn ice. So, here we are, we've come to it,

the easy crossing. Uneasy now, we idle, rereading
the sign. Ah, Henry, what have we combusted

with your engine, in the name
of getting here faster?

Priest in a coffee shop

Priests make the devout and ex-devout alike
nervous, and they worry the non-believer. What
is the use of a priest? said the priest stirring
sadly his coffee. She was opposite

holding her scepticism. On receiving the truth
of his confession she bowed to her cell
phone which was hymning. A message lay
in her psalm. But what's the use? Pray tell.

Ice diver

O feed more salt to that deepsea heart –
blind, propulsive, without a shell, at
each squeeze pushed hard into the net.

Not you, fisherboy, winding in your reel,
sticking to your quota. But you, off-duty,
shoreless, out of your depth, taking your soul

for a freshwater swim under ice, who'll
ascend your bubblebreath trail
in holy isolation. You in a dazzle

of danger, drifting with the light-struck
dead. You, hooded, sealed in your drysuit
habit. Monk, sprinkle the salt.

Speech

The auditorium packed and all their faces
upturned, emptied, stopped. It put me in mind
of the day (it was high summer and I was fifteen)
a school of flounder tried to slip the gap between Kāpiti
and the iron-grey shore   and all were netted and lay
tarnish-eyed, dull-silvered, gills agape.

We strolled among them, harvesting.
Friends and strangers flocked. Sacks
were filled, and baskets. Much of what
we hauled in we gave away. By nightfall
it remained only to pick the net clean of weed
and check for tears and tip the guts

back to the sea. Then home. The triumphant easy win.
The sadness.   I stood. I cleared my throat, began.

Lunch poem for Larry

i.m. Larry Matthews

I'm thinking about this skirt in the op shop when
the bell rings and a customer comes in

and says to the woman behind the counter
Larry is dead.   Walking home

the rain drums on my pink umbrella
and I think, but Larry, but Larry.

I'm walking with Larry *without Larry*
up Stafford Street, up High, past mansion

after mansion – *has many mansions* –
through the green dripping trees – *oh Lana Turner*

we love you, GET UP – hearing Larry read
his ballroom poem, the one that drifted

to the café ceiling: chandelier poem, pendants
dust-mantled and tinkling behind chitchat

long after Larry sat down, its candle-cups
never rewired for electricity, its tapers

playing shadows on our shapes below –
and *happy as*, Larry the magic man on George Street

an audience gathered round   his smile
and up the stairs to late night Larry at his piano

tumbling note upon note into his black
gallery while we looked for pictures in the dark –

          No Larry.
No, Larry.

– and on via a glade where the track bends, that place
always filled with singing birds. *GET UP.*

Wasp

Wasp in the woodpile nests invisible, enters
house in a split pine cradle. Man sets Wasp
in resin-scented basket. Fireside, Wasp snoozes.

Wasp wakes. Groggy, bemused, Wasp emerges.
Wasp circles. Wasp bashes into light fittings,
blunders over cushions and children.

Man hefts several texts, tests each for best flex.
Man climbs to top of couch. Kiddies gasp.
Man sways. Man aims. Man swings. Man stings.

Man holds Wasp by one wing. Man opens
burner door, drops Wasp in. Brief blaze
briefly pleases. A good wasp is a crisp wasp

says Wife. Once we hustled mammoths off cliffs
says Man, amazed, feeling his blood still up.

Pray

One: turn off the phone. Two: kneel.
Three: close the eyes. Four: wait.

Yes, it's difficult. Things to do, places to go.
Hang in there. Sooner or later (probably later)

your god will part the clouds and extend
an empty plate. Chances are you won't

notice straight away (gods are quiet).
Give no money. Behind your shirt pocket

sits another pocket (it might be buttoned down;
the zip might be stuck). Work it open. Reach inside.

Grope around until you've a handful of *it:*
the muck, the lump, the pain, the hollow. Lift it out.

The question is, what is it? It's a question. Place it
on the plate. Now (doubtless the hardest part): wait.

Under	Over
the diver	when he
enters	births himself
the O	bubble
on the ice	by bubble
	up to
descends	O
through	dry light
ice-light	
	he is
so beautiful	thumpingly
it takes	mammalian
his breath	
away	his skin his lungs his heart his blood
so hostile –	and for a while
it could –	
take his –	O!
breath –	
away –	each
	inhalation
he	is
hears	glorious
his	
tubed	each exhalation
air	is
roar	an exultation

Dune din

grain upon grain grain gains upon grain
upon grain upon grain upon grain up on
grain rain rains upon grain shifts grain
up on grain lifts grain up on grain upon
grain upon grain *shhhh* whispers grain
hisses grain and again grain gains upon grain
booms grain upon grain sings grain again grain

Every hunter and forager

Carl Sagan, *Pale Blue Dot*

The sea lion smacks the salmon on the surface of the sea,
whacks it, cracks it, chomps it into pieces. The chunks fly,
pink and silver, pretty on a backdrop of blue.

Blue is the last colour to be named in any language
and we go on knowing it namelessly, for how to say
our primal floating element, so all, so elusive?

No longer solid, the sea opens and the fish falls in.

Admission

From the door you watch him suck in oxygen,
you guess the same concerted way he used to draw down
nicotine from cigarettes, his lips in purse. You see him
drowning in his mask. You see this cannot last.
You knock and enter, introduce yourself. You ask
if you can talk. He bobs more frantically, a gagged
and gagging *if you must*. You ease the mask
from where it grips his face. You put it back
exactly where it was, but now
the air is freed. You check the dial. You lift
and drop the tubing. You sit, you smile. You wait.
And he, he musters up a little chat, old flirt. The man
he is, or was, you greet. You let slide past. You list
the questions: name, age, next of kin, his allergies …

he knows the drill; this has always been the form,
with every nurse who's come before to let him in,
even the burned out, pissed off, steel-jawed ones. Who
are not you. You call him by his name, you listen hard
and if his answer's indistinct you shift the misted mask
to read his lips. You reach the final question, pause.
You lay your pen across your clipboard, raise
your eyes to his. There is between you utter gravitas.
You say your line: 'In the event of … do you want …?'
The words are bald and naked in the room. *Collapse.*
Resuscitation. I watch my father dive down deep. He grasps
his breath and heaves it up to shore. He speaks
as clearly as the bell that someone soon will press
and press and press. 'Thank you. No. I would prefer to rest.'

Unspooling

You think from now on you'll cast each line a little farther into the river,
perhaps as far as the slow pool under the opposite bank where surely
the granddaddy trout swims in place. You think you'll dimple the fly

to the exact gloss centre of that shadow, and let it drift at the insistence
of the current, that dark, invisible insistence. You tell yourself it's time to stretch.
But though you think you'll drop the fly just so, you've failed to factor in

the snags, the weeping willow or the droop-wired fence, and furthermore
your arm is weak, your aim is poor. Three days you spend
at the river, tangles and knots and nothing netted. So now you think

you'll try a new tack, string and a hot-glue gun to make a diamond
kite from newsprint on a balsa frame; and over lunch you read
your sky-bound horoscope which predicts difficulties in all spheres

due to the planets pointing directly at you, so you crack
the calcified head of an egg and eat soldiers spread
with Marmite and dipped in yolk (*alas*, you think, *poor Yorrick*)

and fill in the Code Cracker while a storm wind buffets
the house until the headlines on the kite get jumpy, at which point
you think you'll don a woolly hat and wrap up warm and let the wind

do the unwinding and all you'll have to do is brace your feet
into the ground and hold the stick around which you've wound
a string to touch the moon, and this you do: full of wound-up

yet (let's face it) wounded hope, you liberate your kite
into the gull-slip sky – it's taken up, it's flying! Then
it's not

and you wonder if unspooling is, will ever be, your forte,
a question you will never answer since it never ends,
this casting your line on gale or water

this letting it be swept, this suffering it
to veer and snarl, to plunge, to soar,
meander uselessly   to stall

to accept the catch of absence

to reel   reel   reel

Miser

If ever he wakes in the small hours
he hears it: clink, clink. It never occurs
to him that it's his heart –
he's never heard a heart.
And so he lies and counts.
I count, he thinks, I count.

Report

You can't stopper a volcano with dissidents
though this has been tried. You can't silence

a street by hustling your critic at gunpoint
into an unmarked police car, though this

has also been tried. Somewhere else
a daughter doesn't return to the *casa*;

somewhere else a son goes down
through a scream of space or staggers the stone

stairs blindfolded to the soundproof cell.
But you can't mute what his bones will tell.

And here in the free world, here and near,
over the fence and behind your door,

somebody else or somebody dear is kicked
in the kitchen, punched in the hall; somebody close

is silenced by violence, by lies and denial
and if need be by tears. There's blood on the walls

of the rich and the poor. Yet recoil, yet speak.
Caught: by pen, by camera, caught in thought –

tried and caught, and tried in court. Some wrongs
must be fought. No one can silence the report.

Crime seen

They take her to the morgue. They pull back the sheet.
Can you identify? Yes, I know it. It's the marriage.

Yes it's a tad misshapen. Yes, it does look starved.
They ahem. They aha. They point to where it snapped.

She shrugs. Officers, I committed an honesty.
Shadows parry, thrust, withdraw. The naked bulb swings.

We have reason to believe. We have it on good
authority. How do you plead?

She remembers pleading. No. Don't. I beg you.
They eyeball each other, cough; they shift their feet.

For better, Ma'am, for worse. She blinks. She rears.
Gentlemen, since my back's thumped up

against the wall, I give you this. She bares
her windpipe, faded font where the full stop pressed.

Witness how fast they pull up the sheet!
Nothing to see here, Madam. Move along. We're sweet.

Lingua incognita

Some words dwell in the bone, as yet
unassembled. Like the word you want

for Weary of the City, for Soul Tired; the word
you seek for Confusion Where Affection Once Existed

or the single vowel-filled syllable which would accurately render
Sensation of Freefall Generated by Receipt of Terrifying Information.

Down in the bone the word-strands glimmer and ascend
often disordered, often in dreams,

bone-knowledge beating a path through the body to the throat
labouring to enter the alphabet.

Maybe the bones ache.
Maybe the throat.

Your cells your language, occasionally articulate
in a rush of ease, the body clear as wellspring saying this is

The Moment of Illumination When One Allows that Water Yields
    to Rock, and Always Flows

and sometimes the only word to assemble in the throat is Yes
and sometimes the only word to assemble in the throat is No.

Epitaph

The ghost of you shall set
like rimes of frost inside my chest
and never melt, nor quit
me quite, nor give me rest. It's
not easy to recall us at our best.

Wintersight

The sycamore hoists last-leaf yellow parasols
against a clean blue sky. Paper-thin they sun-wink, spin,
twirled as if by flirting girls commanding an admiring eye.

Gust by gust the parasols are sheared and fall – last leaves,
last leaves after all. The southerly lays stark a graphite sketch
of tree. Comes a solstice low-light gloom when what was once

blocked out is now blocked in: inverse, odd, a widdershins
perspective. In wintersight the iris widens slowly, disbelieving.
Loom into view, like hidden erstwhile constant moons,

the silent, dark and necessary forces: muons, hadrons, gravitons,
charm and strange and love. Can't see by bright what shores us up
or orbits us, what shapes the edges of the known and needed world.

Let parasols be wrecked in soonest storm and let them drop.
Tree be tree and branch be branch. Lean, lean, into the spaces between.

Matariki in the Chinese Garden

1. Batwing

In this defoliated light one sees the careful architecture
of wall, window, roof, path, bridge. One sees, plainly,

the confronting thinness of a tree. The raw
irreducibility of winter startles. This most honest

of seasons, this most exposed. One takes light
where one finds it, which is by dark. *I am*

the world says a pebble in the underfoot batwing.
I am the world, echoes the empty hexagon window.

2. Three irises

Here by the sluicing waterfall
three irises stem from gravel,

lift vermillion stamens to pale sun,
gift a petal hastening on our slow de-hibernation.

Here by the water's flow it starts
again: the turn towards, the upthrust.

Stepping across Zig Zag Bridge

Lan Yuan (A Garden of Distant Longing), Dunedin Chinese Garden

Yellow tassels sway under plum-plump lanterns.
Willow tresses sway. A single yellow lily blooms

        and blooms in the lake, shaking. The lake's
        a green scroll. The calligrapher's hand wavers.

Willow tresses, crimson plums, yellow tassels
waver in the lake. The rocks shake out a waterfall. It falls

        into its shaking self, among
        the rocking peaks where fire-fish ember lazy

trailing feathery fins, fine quills pulling green ink-water
through coiling and uncoiling clouds. The pavilion's

        overlapping clay tile scales upcurl: arched carp,
        leaping. In plunge, the same scales quiver. Pavilion,

illusion of pavilion. Everything exists, and is
imagined. Everything is anchored, and shifts.

        Lattice shadows shift, enclosing
        and disclosing, fluidly disclosing. Stone-twists

open canyons. The longer one stays by the green water
the more one sees. So at full moon, the moon in the lake

        rises in the lake, lilts on the lake, pours
        through the hand. Fire-fish sip from its rim.

New book

Ruffle the pages and think of a yawning woman
ruffling the hair on her scalp, sleepy, dream-clogged,
coming back to her day self. Her spine cracks

and so too, waking, stretched, this book's.
So too solidify the nouns we live with –
chair, bed, cat, cup, window, door –

so too the busy verbs get cracking; so too
the sentence shrugs on ink and snakes a path
beyond. Once upon,

and next and then and next and then
and then and then The End. In which
is our beginning. Ruffle the pages and

Forgiveness

Forgiveness. Such a pretty word, for such a bitch.
A misnomer, like dropping Patience or Prudence
on the brow of a soft babe held over a stone font
who grows up an impulsive, careless cunt.
Forgiveness is all claws. She won't come to my call
but nor will she shake loose. She has me in maul.
Most mornings, 3 a.m., she speaks. You can't give me away
she says. Nor am I for sale. If you want to use my name
to settle debts and soothe your pain, you'll pay. I'll have the wring
of you, you'll twist and shout before you sing
the bad-good song, the did-no-wrong, the put-it-all-
behind-us-now-move-on. My job's to prowl
your mind and heart and scratch up squirts of acid.
Not until you're out of stink will I be placid.

Sea foam at Gemstone Beach

Yellow sea foam is emerging from the ocean, wave
upon wave of jelly-creatures slithering from salt
to shore. Here it comes, a species long cradled in the deep,
shedding fathoms, shedding sea-water, not yet limbed for land.

Spongy-looking, lung-like. On they come. Quivering,
shuddering, sucking at gravity, light, the searing wind.
Never has there been such pain. Excruciating. Addictive.
They must! They must! They will! They will!

They scud, they skate, and each metre more onto the beach
is another bone cell imagining itself out of jelly. Is this joy?
It is joy! Shake, shake! Jelly-creatures conquer the world!
Until the sandbank, its small wall studded with gemstones.

Quartz, topaz, amethyst. Earth-kilned, earth-polished,
each is reversing out of land. Not so as you'd notice, but
plop, plop, eon by eon, they are falling back to the beach.
Still the yellow sea foam comes, and piles in a wobble

at the barrier, puzzling at solidity. Concentrate! Concentrate!
Wings? Wings! The first shreds fly up and over.

An international poetry festival in Vietnam

The authorities are nervous. It's risky
to bring in the poets. When they say *flower*
are they speaking of flowers?

It's risky for the poets. It can lame a poet,
bearing these poems. They are avid, intent. Absorbed,
absorbing and their poems fatten, loom.

When they recite they offer words like flowers
if the flowers were strewn like limbs
and the limbs reclaimed

and the bones ground
in a mortar with the spit of the ancestors
ground and ground with a heavy granite pestle

so as to dissolve under the tongue
of the enemy, so as to restart the heart.

Strange monster

'We who are writing women and strange monsters' – May Sarton

She wields a potato peeler. She peels
and pares, pares and peels. Apple-skin
falls in the sink. Broken coils,

discontinuous scroll which no longer reads
apple. Unnameable mound thing, mounding.
Twigs, leaves, that dead red hat

stuck in a grate at the bottom of the street. A mound
undoing its yarn, retreating to before the idea
of hat on the needle's nib went knitting.

Moss, pearl, garter, rib. To before the ball.
Carriage in a pumpkin seed, footman in a green lizard.
She'll take this skin to the worms, let them compose it,

beautiful scribblers. Black inscriptions
on a black page darkly. She slips
down a wormhole, squirms up a week ago

leaning into a bedlam wind, powerlines
heaving, bin-scud, sky-roar, as if the storm
has the city by the scruff and shakes it

but – ha! – that dog, steady spaniel, upright
on a neat lawn, nose in the nor'wester
(nose in a novel, sunshine on a window seat)

tracking howling hunger across oceans,
engrossed in some family saga imprinted
in a code of salts blown in on the gale.

Oh, to have the dog's discerning nose,
to discriminate more wisely the good apple
from the bad.   Rinse.

Cool sluiced fingers, the juice swirls and dives.
She lines up pale, bald heads, chooses
a blade. Kitchen tools: Marianne Moore

kept an auger, two axes and a gimlet
on a singular rack of her own construction.
Burble-burble mutters the chutney.

Stir.

She would have a wooden spoon and tongs.
A knife. A sharp pen. Take down this incessant simmer
where the words form and dissolve, sometimes

plunge so fast and deep, irretrievable, the notebook
so often a room away, out of the steam. Strange
monster. Licks for that vinegar chilli zip. Spices

and a hot flame, the pot's soft plops and a pungency
filling the kitchen. This, her cabbage talk. This, her sauce,
her relish. This habitually her plain, stern face

leaning and tending and making. The distance, she must tell
her children, between say and do's the thing. And fine words
butter no parsnips, nor divvy a cabbage for slaw. And

watch their hands, my darlings, as the gentlemen go by.
Sets out the jars. Boils the jug. Now she's called.
And answers, always answers. Has to, in the end.

Barrel organ out of order

'Our imagination being like a barrel organ out of order, that always plays some other tune than that shown on its card ...' – Marcel Proust, *In Search of Lost Time*

The barrel organ's waltzing and the organ grinder's humming
and up and down the street the windows are flung open
and canaries chirp in cages and ladies lean out smiling,

> Princess This and Princess That, made royal by the organ grinder's song;
> and patting spotted headscarves into high-plumed velvet turbans
> and swinging hand-laced petticoats (not tatty cotton aprons)

they lean upon the sills as if their breasts might spill from all constraint,
and the kids scoot up with pennies for the organ grinder's supper
with grubby knees and urchin grins and shiny eyes

> as polished as that far-off sprung-floored ballroom
> on which one day in silk and tails they'll swirl, they'll twirl –
> for love, for love, for love –

like mama in the window as the barrel organ sings it,
gliding in her taffetas, her diamond ear drops twinkling,
as the monkey spies a gentleman and clambers off the barrel,

> whips a crown from noble wallet, slips it monkey-waistcoat pocket
> and scales the organ grinder to perch haughty on his shoulder,
> as the children's laughter rings and the ladies fan their faces,

as for mirth and flirt and happenstance they waltz,
as the barrel card reads poverty but rolls this dream,
this one, two, three. Completely out of order. Praise be.

Abandoned stable, Matanaka

A whinny-wind blows through the cracks
and hay-whiff hits and   I remember

     misted morning rides on horse-wide tracks
     on board the felted ribcage of a breathing beast.
     Seed heads swashed our knees. We parted leaves.
     The passing world itched flesh to snort and snicker.
     Ears flick-flicked and swivelled: nets set to catch
     the pitch of tremors set off by a distant barking dog.
     The bite, the bit, the spit, the froth, the foam.
     The lips that curled back rubbery to show
     the sea-slug tongue, the yellow chomping bones.
     The mahogany eye held mine, and mine
     was small. The saddle was my tiny *terra firma*.
     An ocean poured beneath according to its tides
     and drifts, its currents, counter-currents, sway,
     its shifts and twitch and slip. Apple, midge,
     a thunder clap. It was a riding with, or it was
     riding braced, against.
               When we shared the wind for comb,
     when we adjusted each to each: shin to flank, eye
     to eye and shoe for shoe. When empty tank
     was hunger, rest; when mileage was a trail of steaming piles.

Empty stable. Derelict. But clop-clop-clops a broken board
and nickers tin   and hay-whiff hits
and ancestry kicks into stirrup and I (who never rode) remember –
goes giddy-up my blood, my blood, my blood.

Three poems at the well

(i) Wishes

I had a red coat and a cold coin.
I was naked from the cuffs down.
A thin wind nipped my wrists raw.
I was the oldest sister, not the beautiful one
and so I hefted myself up to see over
the lip of the well. At first I saw wishes
in the water, and then I saw the wreck
of them plain, a scattering of small change
under the floating popsicle sticks,
a mesh across the throat to keep
us kids from falling for it. Wishful

thinking. Time to go. I was holding up the show.
With my dreaming, with my slow. So the giants
said, calling from the gates at the edge of the park.

(ii) Pipe dream

My feet roll on cut-up tyres. On my head,
a tin tub. My daughter's hat is a faded bucket.

Her sandals don't match: one blue, one black,
one short, one long, the buckles gone.

Slap. Slap.

We pass the Coca Cola sign and we pass
under the red gaze of dusty gunboys.

No laughter at the well. No wish
but the wish about the belly pains of our babies,

our babies whose eyes don't blink, who loll incurious
in our wraps. Must they drink parasites,

our ancient, withered babies? If we could wash.
If we could cleanly slake our thirst. A cascade

then, of beautiful downstream consequences,
like literacy, like *well*.

(iii) Golden balls

The princess would have had more fun
if she had thrown the ball again, sending
the frog to fetch and fetch and fetch.

That way she could have got on with her work
as that man there, reading under a tree,
is getting on with his, absentmindedly

tossing a stick for his dog, who capers
back and forth, repeatedly snuffling it out
and, bringing it to his hand, drops, sits, waits.

Of animals

Children are inhabited by animals: tiger, lion, bear.
Nothing they've ever seen in the flesh,
but roaring, but clawing, but fangs, fur,
fins, feathers, fear. Dinosaurs inhabit them,
and wolves and sharks. Blue whales,
killer whales. Dolphin, unicorn, coyote, fox.

Animals inhabit them until they inhibit
the animals, inhabit the uniform, achieve
the standards, become adults, accumulate,
accommodate. The animals hibernate.
Hot breath builds in the blocked black cave.
When the animals wake they are parched and famished.
They howl, they gnash. Naturally, they roam and hunt.

A treatise on the benefits of moonbathing

All insomnias, whether reactive, endogenous or apostrophe-induced, respond well to moonbathing, which raises levels of vitamin M in the blood. – *Luna Medicine Quarterly*

Moonbathing, one glows.
One becomes (if nude)
a composition of orbs, variously lit, according to phase.

Every season's good if the weather's fine.

A harvest moonbathe in an apple orchard
within earshot of the sea is always pleasant (ah, the lunar seas)

Mare Crisium
Oceanus Procellarum

as is the sharp shiver when one divests oneself of winceyette at midnight
under a halo of ice

and even better the escapade in snow
two thousand feet above worry level with the moon's smile sailing over the forest

Mare Frigoris.

A moonbath in spring is a spritz to the hibernated soul.
One skips back, freshly rinsed
with sparkling thoughts like *moonwash gilds us all the same, O our beautiful bones!*

Mare Nectaris.

Then those longest shortest nights in itch-hot sheets
tick toss tick toss tick toss tick toss

until at last
you step out barefoot on the silver grass

balmed, becalmed, singing psalms
under that old rocket parking lot.

Mare Tranquillitatis.

Scientists say most of us have a deficiency.

Therefore, moon on, mooncalf under a moon dog drinking moonshine –

Mare Serenitatis.
Mare Luminescum.

Snow flurry on York Place

Thought that it was blossom drifting past but it was snow.
Was wrapped for June of course, but not for *snow*. Zing
still in my mouth from grapes I'd nicked moments ago,
those tiny grapes that grow against the wall on Ross and Bruce
half-hidden in the straggly vine. A plum tree mocking up
its petals there, that's what I'd carried with me in my mind
and so, on York, these flakes, I think them blossom, and only
turn them slow in alteration … so, it's snow? … A door
lets out a little girl, her mother. How a snowflake falls,
it's unmistakeable, a kind of flight as if intention drives it, or maybe
bliss, a giving up control. 'Oh! Snow!' They make the sign
of open-fingered catching: this show's about to start, and tickets free
and would you look at us – the ringside seats. We beam, strangers
being snowed upon together. Duchesses. Blow some, storm, and more.

Bound

It nosed into the traffic like a shark
insinuating its way into a school of sardines
and away we cruised, the hearse
and I, side by side, catching the green
the length of the one way, past the museum park
where a bevy of long-legged fake-tans
was waiting to cross, past
the hospital, the chocolate factory and the supermarket, past
the station and the clicking tourists, past
Toitū with its walls of early settlers. At the cenotaph
our paths diverged, at last. Not far beyond I passed
a girl who shook her hair down in the sun, and laughed.

Graveyard poem

In a cemetery in sunlight with names
wept into granite, I lie on a grave

under a defoliating oak, crisp leaves
flittering. Concrete cold creeps

into my spine, aligns me with death. But
the sun's warm yet. You sit

on the neighbour's tomb, you wait,
and quietly we listen to the trees' last-minute discussions.

Then we walk, past all the men in their sunken plots, dear morning
beards, and the yews twisting roots through their bones;

all the graves on a slope so steep the lids
might slip off like toboggans should it snow;

all the wives adored or endured, corseted or cosseted,
whose costal cartilages smile whitely, deep in the dirt;

all the children with their terrifying ages engraved stark against bewilderment –

it's right to be so afraid
of love.

We walk. We wend past the mossy graves on soft earth
which takes our footprints in and gives them back, a little bounce

and the green words chant on the tombstones
dearly beloved, deeply cherished,

and the angels dip their wingtips to our occasionally touching palms
and the leaves rustle underfoot: risk it, risk it.

Central

Hoar frost on a high road.
Then we're through: Central.

Far sun. Close moon.
Cloud stitched tight

to the still lake's brim. We
lie down on the shingle shore,

apply silence, balm
our selves. A bird

beats over. At first sight
alone, such respect

has its companion
for solitude. At wide arc,

the other. A sure-winged
homing. Each, to the other, central.

At Hawea

Only these particular noon winter solstice raindrops
primed by a year of quake, eruption and eclipse

could compose exactly this: to round the corner
of the lake and find it chiming,

bubbles doming the surface, gliding there
like a fleet of glass cupolas.

Struck, they ring and die,
ring and ring under rain in the mountain bowl.

This peculiar percussion to call this bay
to bell so true, so close to a sob. And only now

to hold one's breath for fear of breaking
this aligned specific tension,

this enchantment, spell, this
                    what planets do.

Black Lake

The bones that lie around Black Lake are lichen spotted.
They do not gleam. They are not white.
Not the idea of bone, but bone itself, scattered, split.

The mist that rises from Black Lake, like steam
as if the water boiled, is strangled smoke. What burns
burns deep without the grace of oxygen. It smoulders.

The insects stalking on Black Lake are unaware
how thin the membrane; the fish that swim there
can't be seen; the eels are blind. The lake eats light

spits nothing back. Reeds are weathered, withered,
wizened. Birds don't sing, and wing-bound, no bird
flies. Whoever walks at Black Lake

walks in peril. Who comes back, comes back broken,
comes back stronger, glued, resized.

Poem to my nearest galaxy

Yes, I had forsaken curiosity, let it
dull. Now, a most delicate bell,
it chimes as if a monk at meditation's
end gently tapped the brass, a call

to wake. Stirred. Beguiled.
Not simply interested. Agog. The stars
above (if they're above) recede
in an ever expanding universe

and here by your side at midnight
I'm startled childish by wonder.
Galaxies? Infinite question, red-shift
reply. But you, you helped me remember.

Daffodils

You couldn't call them seasonal. Rain
has never touched them. And as for hail
or snow … No, this is their first breeze,

this shift of stale air as a child runs past.
They can't nod in it. They didn't learn in grass.
They wear tight headscarves, more green than gold,

and stare down, down, into the bucket.
They don't trumpet. Yet, that jolt, that reminder.
Hillary, I haven't forgotten. Your voice

was hoarse and low. It hurt
to talk by then. I let myself in. So straight
you had to sit, propped by all those cushions.

Your porridge was long cold in the bowl,
cold tea brimmed a floral cup. How I lurched,
off-balance, flinging words at you, plumping

the pillows, whisking away the porridge, whizzing
up a juice, pressing the glass into your hand.
Insisting, fussing, gossiping.

Your velvet Afghan hat that hugged your scalp.
I said *I really like your hat*
and I touched it. Your stillness as I bustled.

And all the while, invisibly, under the lawn
the daffodils were putting on a spurt. You, days
and nights in a high-backed chair at the window

knew of this. Your world had opened, relaxed.
I, of course, was shocked, after you died,
that spring could be so callous, so loud, so, so …

trumpeting. These thrawn supermarket buds,
they remind me. *Don't wait,* you said,
the only urgent words you ever spoke to me.

This was thirteen sweeps of the sun ago. Hillary,
I have never forgotten. When the true daffodils
re-emerge this season (I believe I hear them rising)

I will bend to the soil in gratitude. Your legacy,
your bequest. Yes, Hillary – I did. I grabbed my life.

Calling

We let the string sleep slack between our houses
hours, days, years, until one of us tugs.
Then, lifted and pulled taut, we speak. Buzz
words coming down the line. A baked bean can
for trumpet and for conch. Our voices echo sound,
plumbing the marks. On my lips, your name, a manner
of holding you and what you spell. Something like
kin and kinship, something like kind; something *like*,
affection being the grounding stitch of love, which,
purl to plain and slip-one-pass-one-over, knits
our kith. Peculiar patterns we make
with our yarn, shaped to what blows through and what's
prevailing. Rambunctious winds, or fretful. These times
you are bent beneath a howling. I am picking up
the string to make a steady tether for your heart.
For thy heart. Dear friend, I'm thinking of thee.

A day trip to the peninsula

(i)
The kingfisher doesn't budge from the wire,
though we kick up gravel dust with our wheels, though
we sound like a thousand buffaloes.

Never having heard a thousand buffaloes, but familiar
with traffic on that unsealed road which borders its lagoon,
the kingfisher does not swivel its head.

Its one concern is for the water. Tide-filled, serene,
everything is doubled: boatshed, wire and kingfisher
in perfect symmetry. Nothing moves

in the lagoon, or nothing upon which the kingfisher cares
to comment. It's so mild it's difficult
to believe this is the first day of winter. The sun

is in the water shining up, and regal fishes
swim across it, and we ungainly drive
into the picture, are reflected in the shallows as we pass.

(ii)

Pūkeko steps out of the verge.
Unhurried, stately, it embarks upon
the dry strip that bisects its wetland territory,
struts across. Blue cloud on stilts
which does not deign to glance.

Pūkeko descends into the opposite ditch,
vanishes. The fringes close, not
as bead curtains or macramé tassels
swish, but as a door to which we have
no key, no word, no code. Pūkeko walks on.

(iii)

A hawk flies out of the hillside and swoops
over the ground we stand on. Slow, and low,

cumbersomely braking, dropping back
from swift to first, trundling its shadow

like a taloned plough across the paddock,
crooning the soil: come, soar.

We see flight feathers flare
and adjust, could stroke

the soft stripes on its underbelly. Hawk
takes in the fact of us. Hawk

sweeps on. Its eye is tacked to the grass,
to the story written in it. Something about

small creatures startled out of hiding;
something scribbled in a shiver.

(iv)

We park under the old man pines, and cross the stile.
Needles shift underfoot   then sand. The track

narrows and ascends the dune. The lupins
are green and winter-soft. They don't scratch

where we fumble through. They have forgotten
their high-heat pod-snap   and we have forgotten

this roar   always we forget   always we become
muffled. But this reverberation   bone-rumble   then we crest

and there's the sight of it: salt-haze over the surf,
the breakers in coil and spritz   sand curve gleaming.

Loud. We walk into the din and light of it.

(v)

Our skins with the day still on them tingle
in the sheets. Interstitial, hovering, the road
rocks the bed. Something about reeds,
barely shifting, something about a jewel-blue
cloud, something about a wide
sky, wade. Something about close
and closing, a line stretched over the lagoon.
Soar, light on water. Something about shiver.

Our salts prickle in their rivulets.

Mist

'We should live, my Lesbia, we should love' – Catullus V

Mist cloaked the hill and house all day
and would not shift. Lest this
be misperceived: what bliss. The hush
of barely falling rain upon a roof; the wall
of yellow-gold wisteria just stirring itself
to nod. Once or twice a starling whooshed across
and vanished. Whether all was
gloom or loom or luminescence
who could tell? Not us. No shadows, thus
no rush. Nothing to see beyond the fence.
We hung suspended in our cloud. Chores
complete and leisure leisurely consumed,
there still remained what we two never missed.
We pulled each other close. We kissed.

The crop

Massed up against the garden wall, the canes
are heavy, laden. Her hands part stalks and dive
through leaves, seeking deeper harvest. Strands
of currants swing against her wrist, glass-bead bright.
As to how they're lit, is it from within, or from without?
This puzzle dazzles, or is that this dazzle puzzles?

Her hands work on. Drop by drop she picks the crop – she
and She: Someone She, millennia-gone, who honed
this pincer grip on something-berries, and she,
unforeseeable by She, who stands now in the beds,
stripping the glut for jelly. The fruit mounds in the colander
like a placenta. Scarlet juice stains all her fingers.

She prints the wall. One day another She will come
when it is winter and the canes are bare and she is gone.

Little shanty

My hull, my anchor and my sail,
my spinnaker, my mizzen,
my oars and rudder, cyclone, swell –
my ocean, my horizon.

My reach, my catch, my rum, my junk,
ahoy, awash, athwart,
my fore, my aft, my wreck, my keel,
my starboard tack, my list to port.

Let ships be tossed, let tempests roar,
so rough and wild the sea,
you're my lantern, I'm your shore –
fair wind speed you home to me.

Luff and lee and sink or swim,
my offshore breeze and keen sea wind,
scurvy, scupper, schooner, stern,
my able-bodied seaman.

My captain, crew and cabin boy,
my passenger, my mate,
my compass, chart, crow's nest, my raft,
reef and bay and strait.

Let ships be tossed, let tempests roar,
so rough and wild the sea,
you're my lantern, I'm your shore –
fair wind speed you home to me.

Round turn and two half hitches,
bowline, sheepshank, sloop.
Up the channel, round the Horn,
Panama, Good Hope.

My mast, my deck, my figurehead,
my galley slave, my freighter,
my porthole, sextant, lifeboat, salt,
my Plimsoll line, Equator.

My longitude, my latitude,
safe harbour, jig and hold.
Capsized, rescued, drowned and saved,
my pirate's chest of gold.

Let ships be tossed, let tempests roar,
so rough and wild the sea,
you're my lantern, I'm your shore –
fair wind speed you home to me.

Smeuse

(Sussex dialect noun: the gap in the base of a hedge made by the regular passage of a small animal)

Something there is that loves a hedge. Something there is
that snouts an underleaf and commutes. Something there
is prickle-backed, slate-tiled or merely vertebral –

fur blanket over chain-link bone – something belly-soft
and sniffy, something hungry for a grub, that can forage,
that can hunker nested twig-down low in ice, reduced,

that spring-blooms up with sex flowers ripe and dangling –
plums and strutting, plumage, rutting – something gleams,
persists. Some summer thing there is, hankering for shade.

Some things there are that slip between properties,
dirt-pawed, star-whiskered, articulate in scent,
fluent in the zillion dialects of air, some things

chatting to each other as if we don't exist, us without
antennae, us with our attenuated octaves, our day-set
rods and cones, bald us, our goose bumps all for show that fail

to raise our quills, us who wall the hedges, stop
the smeuse.
        Something there is will disregard the bipeds.

Some deep-time thing imagination can't imagine
without the garden's little creatures making gaps
and smeusing. Something there is that loves a hedge,

that does not hedge – that will not shilly-shally, bet –
but makes a passage just its size and shuttles
back and forth. Something there is.

Luthier

He has the guitar in mind. In his quake-rocked studio he leans
over the quiet grain. Listen: rain falling on Vancouver Island.
Six flitches of Sitka spruce with which to summon sound.

This spruce conducted breeze and storm for centuries,
never knew a day to pass in silence, recognised her guests
by footfall and by wing-rush: squirrel scurry, spiral of ants

on the sap route, beaks and claws and paws, all that
patter and flutter and slink. Summer-heated cones clicked
open, slow-baked, while the high tips waltzed

close to the sun; and in blind winter the whole tree
threshed, screaming *Alaska* at the gale until the branches
bowed to the weight of a white, creaking shush. This

for a thousand thousand moons. A brief age then:
of rumbling, of shouts and engines and a bedrock shimmering
that teased loose the grip of roots, and briefer still

the day   and very brief the act   and when the act was done, the wood
was mute. He splits each flitch and pauses. He hears the stuck
scratch of needle-sharp leaves upon a long-gone sky.

He has the guitar in mind and in hand. He leans over the polished
grain. He loves the shape of her, he loves her song. Listen:
rain falling on Vancouver Island. His fingers threading strings.

Living above the croquet club

Often in summer they're there by the time I rise –
as if they sprouted, mushroom-like, overnight
or are stilt-legged seabirds studding an estuary –
still and stooped over their hoops
singly or in pairs, white on the immaculate green.

And if I am granted the grace and the moment
before I turn from the bright window to walk down
into the morning, there comes the crack of the shot
and the slow ballet of their repositioning.
With calm accuracy may today be blessed.

The yield

Despite the silver label braceletting
that slender limb, that's no Belle de Boskoop.
It's come out different, come out all itself,
whatever itself is, proud to bear
boughs freighted, not with yellow apples, blushed,
but with fine stripes of russet, lemon, lime.
Tart and crisp, delicious. Mystifying.
But not the first surprise it's sprung on me.
The first surprise was simply that it lived,
that dehydrated sapling, just a stick,
uprooted from a silt-fed infancy,
rejected from re-designated soil.
I heeled it in and watered it, more from
courtesy than hope. Then I forgot it.

Earth rolled us slowly out of darkness. Buds
swelled. A cloud of blossom flared. Soon bees
zizzed back and forth, danced loop-de-loops. It had
pulled through, albeit crooked, not ideal.
Inadequately staked, it had developed
a lean, the whole tree on an angle,
as if surrendering in deference
to persistent pressure, as if leaned upon,
giving in or giving up to what prevails,
what pushes, presses louder, stronger, most
insistently. Forced to a stiffened warp,
its thwarted stoop sad manifesto for
survival: appeasement, resignation,
a growing into being out of whack.

Or see the tree withstanding: letting go
to put out arms, become a fruitful crux,

unshackled by the piece of tin that calls
it Belle. It's come out in commitment to
the quest for light, and this has shaped it, fired
it upwards; this has driven down the roots
to grasp the unfamiliar clay. Criss-crossed
constantly by stars and worms, so bonded
to this place and bending to it, as ice
melts in its season, streams away. It's ridden
home by riding its own pliant power.
It's found its truest way to skew. And now
the triumph of this quietly blazing show.
It yields and from the yield all flows.

ACKNOWLEDGEMENTS AND NOTES

Thank you to Emma Neale and Fiona Moffat for astute editing and design. I'm grateful for the loving support of my family and friends, especially Laurence Fearnley, intelligent reader and wise friend throughout the writing of this collection.

Versions of some of these poems have been previously published in the following periodicals: *Aesthetica* (UK); *Deep South*; *Island* (Tasmania, Australia); *Atlanta Review* (USA); *JAAM*; *Hippocrates Prize Anthology* 2013 and 2016; *Landfall*; *London Grip*; NZ Poetry Society Anthologies *Ice Diver*, *Take Back Our Sky* and *Scattered Feathers*; *Otago Daily Times*; *Poetry New Zealand*; *Shenandoah* 61 (USA); *Takahē*; *The Press* (Christchurch); *Tremble* (University of Canberra Vice-Chancellor's Poetry Prize anthology 2016); *Turbine*; *Underneath* (University of Canberra Vice-Chancellor's Poetry Prize anthology 2015).

'Matariki in the Chinese Garden' and 'Stepping across Zig Zag Bridge' were previously published in *Lan Yuan: A Garden of Distant Longing* (Dunedin: Dunedin Chinese Gardens Trust and Shanghai Museum, 2013).

'Jar' was first published in *Out of Shape* (Canberra: Ampersand Duck, 2014), a letterpress collection designed, hand-set and printed by Caren Florance.

'A treatise on the benefits of moonbathing' is for Paula Green.

'Snow flurry on York Place' is dedicated to Laura and Grace Cope – no longer strangers.

'Strange monster' was longlisted for the 2016 University of Canberra Vice-Chancellor's International Poetry Prize.

'Calling' won the 2015 *Takahē* Poetry Competition.

'Luthier' won the 2015 Caselberg Trust International Poetry Prize. This poem is dedicated to Christchurch-based luthier and guitarist Graham Wardrop.

'The yield' was longlisted for the 2015 University of Canberra Vice-Chancellor's International Poetry Prize.

'Smeuse' was runner-up in the 2015 Gwen Harwood Poetry Prize (Tasmania, Australia). This poem is dedicated to Robert Macfarlane who introduced me to 'smeuse' and many other exact but almost forgotten landscape words in his book *Landmark* (London: Hamish Hamilton, 2015).

'Daffodils' won the poetry section in the 2013 Cancer Council Victoria Arts Awards.

'Wild' shared second place in the 2013 International Hippocrates Prize for Poetry and Medicine. This poem is for Carolyn Upton, 1963–2014.

'Ice diver' won the 2011 New Zealand Poetry Society International Competition.

Note to 'Lunch poem for Larry': 'oh Lana Turner we love you get up' is from 'Poem' by Frank O'Hara, in Donald Allen (ed.) *The Collected Poems of Frank O'Hara* (Berkley: University of California Press, 1995).

Notes to 'Strange monster': 'This, her cabbage talk' derives from 'I go out to the kitchen to talk cabbages and habits', from 'In the men's room(s)' by Marge Piercy, in *Eight Chambers of the Heart: Selected Poems,* (London: Penguin, 1995).

'[H]er plain, stern face' derives from 'I sternly accept this plain face', in 'I have had to learn to live with my face' by Diane Wakoski, in *Emerald Ice: Selected Poems 1962–1987* (Jaffrey, New Hampshire: Black Sparrow Press, 2005).

Marianne Moore's 'singular rack of her own construction' and information on the implements therein is from 'Humility, Concentration, and Gusto' by Winthrop Sargeant, first published in *The New Yorker*, 16 Feb 1957.